SICKLE CELL
NATURAL
HEALING

SICKLE CELL NATURAL HEALING

A Mother's Journey

Tamika Moseley

AuthorHouse™ LLC
1663 Liberty Drive
Bloomington, IN 47403
www.authorhouse.com
Phone: 1-800-839-8640

Published by AuthorHouse   10/21/2013

ISBN: 978-1-4918-1391-1 (sc)
ISBN: 978-1-4918-1392-8 (e)

Library of Congress Control Number: 2013916677

Any people depicted in stock imagery provided by Thinkstock are models, and such images are being used for illustrative purposes only. Certain stock imagery © Thinkstock.

This book is printed on acid-free paper.

Introduction

The understanding of sickle cell disease still remains a mystery. As a child in Louisiana growing up with "the trait," I learned from an early age that this life-threatening disease was very serious, and that many children and adults died from sickle cell disease. Even today, sickle cell disease is still very much just as serious as it ever was: people are still suffering with sickle cell disease, living with extreme pain, suffering from strokes, organ failure and more. There are millions of people around the globe affected by this disease.

And while the medical field has come a long way today with studies, trials and testing, for me, I felt there is still not a drug available that will minimize my son's sickle cell crisis without side effects. The only treatment drug available, hydroxyurea, is a very potent drug with many serious side effects and has been known to be fatal in some cases. According to statistics, there are between 70,000-100,000 people suffering from sickle cell disease and two million people with the trait in the United States. In Nigeria, there are between three to five million people affected with sickle cell disease; 200,000 Nigerian infants are born with sickle cell disease and 100,000 of them will die yearly. In Africa, where medical care is in short supply, death rates from sickle cell disease are extremely high.

Because this disease has played such a huge part in my life, I have done extensive research on natural herbs for more than seven years and have discovered natural supplements that really do work. I have also discovered herbs that will minimize sickle cell crises and other problems. Herbs have been used for thousands of years by many cultures to heal all kinds of serious diseases and keep the body healthy and strong. Ancient civilizations used herbs to treat disease thousands of years ago. The history of Indian herb treatment, Ayurveda, is more than 5,000 years old. China, Europe and the Middle East all have a long history of herbal treatments dating back 3,500 years. Today in countries around the world, people rely on herbs for different treatments as well as disease prevention treatment. They are very powerful substances and should be respected as such.

The year 2009 was a very challenging time for my husband Rodney and me. Our one-year-old son, Aiden, was in the hospital every three months with a sickle cell crisis. Each time he was hospitalized for up to two weeks, and he received two blood transfusions that same year. This was a very difficult and emotional time in my family's life. I cried nightly and feared for my son's life. I started treating Aiden with natural herbs in March 2010, when he was two years old. Two years passed without a single incident of sickle cell crisis or any issues related to sickle cell disease. Treating my son's disease with herbs has been one of the smartest decisions I've made in my life. There is no worse torture for a parent than seeing your child in constant pain. Those were emotionally agonizing and heart-wrenching times, and I knew I had to make a change for the sake of his health. I give thanks to God for opening my eyes and directing my steps to care for my son naturally.

This book will explain my personal testimony with my child and the herbs I chose to treat him with. I've written this book to help everyone suffering from sickle cell disease or the trait and to be an inspiration for others. There is an end to the pain. Things can be better and you can enjoy a full, beautiful and happy life living with sickle cell disease.

Chapter 1

My Sickle Cell Experience

I was born in 1974 in Shreveport, Louisiana with the sickle cell trait. Having "the trait" means a person carries only one sickle gene and does not have the disease. Sickle cell trait will not and cannot turn into the full-blown disease, and under usual circumstances, a person with sickle cell trait won't feel sick or be in pain. However, it is very possible to experience symptoms of the disease under extreme conditions of over-exertion, physical stress or decreased oxygen levels. In some cases, people with the trait have gotten extremely sick and even died while playing sports or during pregnancy.

I found out I had the trait at 19 years old. I was in the Army Reserves and had medical issues with one of my legs. During my time on post, I saw several doctors who ran tests on me before releasing me on a medical discharge. A few months later, the Army sent me a letter informing me that I had been diagnosed with sickle cell disease, a fatal disease, and I should seek medical attention immediately.

I found a general physician in the phone book and made an appointment. At that age, I didn't realize I should have been making an appointment with a hematologist, a doctor that specializes in blood disorders and diseases of the blood. The doctor asked me if I was in pain often, and if I was sickly on a regular basis. Because I answered no to both questions, he told me not to worry—people with the trait never experience any difficulties with sickle cell disease and they live normal lives. Later in life, I found out that people with the trait can die, which shocked me.

Sickle cell disease is an inherited blood disease that causes hemoglobin cells to be defective in the red blood cells that carry oxygen to the tissues of the body. This process involves the red blood cells, hemoglobin and their ability to carry oxygen. A normal person's hemoglobin cells are smooth, flexible and round in shape so they can move through our body's blood vessels easily without any problems. Sickle cell hemoglobin cells are sticky, stiff and form a shape of a c, and when they lose oxygen, these cells tend to cluster together and cannot move easily through blood vessels. This cluster causes problems or blockage and it also stops the movement of healthy oxygen carrying blood. When this blockage occurs, this is what causes the painful episodes and other complications of sickle cell disease.

Growing up, I can remember often times having unexplained pain in my arms and legs. My parents had no idea why I was in pain and they didn't know what to do for me, so I suffered through the pain episodes and just became used to hurting. During my basic training in the military, we did physical training every single morning, which puts a lot of stress on the body. I would get exhausted quickly and I didn't understand why. Looking back on my life then, I can understand more clearly why these things were happening to me.

After I was released from the military, I didn't give my sickle cell trait another thought, especially after my Louisiana doctor told me I had nothing to worry about. Thirteen years later, I met a wonderful man, and we dated for a year during which time the subject of sickle cell trait came up. We realized together that not only did I have the trait, but he had SC disease, considered a milder form of sickle cell disease that happens when a person inherits the Hemoglobin C gene and the Hemoglobin S gene. SC disease may cause similar symptoms as SS disease, or full-blown sickle cell disease, but produces less anemia due to a higher blood count level. People with SC generally experience symptoms that are less severe than SS disease, when a child inherits the S gene from both parents. They may suffer from anemia, a condition that reduces the amount of available red blood cells and causes fatigue, or they may have normal levels of red blood cells. They may also have retinopathy, which is acute damage to the retina of the eye, and can experience necrosis of the bone, which is the death of bone tissue due to lack of blood supply. Also called osteonecrosis, avascular necrosis can lead to tiny breaks in the bone until the bone eventually collapses.

I can't remember exactly where we were at that time, but I can remember how that news hit me. We were already in love, yet I considered breaking it off with him because the last thing I wanted was to bring a child into this world with a fatal blood disease. The decision I made was to stay together and let the Lord direct our steps.

At age 33, after a perfect pregnancy, I had my first child, a beautiful baby girl we named Mariah. I had no health issues whatsoever and wanted to have another child right away. The results I received back from the Health Department were that my daughter had the trait, which was a huge relief to my husband and me. We knew that meant Mariah is only a carrier of sickle cell disease and will never have the disease, so she should live a healthy and normal life. She took my A gene and took my husband's C gene, which is called Hemoglobin C trait. People with C trait have red blood cells that have normal hemoglobin A and an abnormal hemoglobin. The abnormal hemoglobin is called hemoglobin C. She has slightly more hemoglobin A than hemoglobin C. Thankfully; people with Hemoglobin C trait do not normally have any health problems related to sickle cell.

In 2007 I was pregnant with my second child and delivered him in 2008. This time the news we received was that my newborn baby had full-blown sickle cell disease, and my life was shattered. Aiden took my S gene and my husband's S gene which gave him SS disease. Two weeks after I delivered, I started having difficulties breathing, experienced shortness of breath and my chest hurt when I would lie down. I called my doctor and she told me to go to the hospital immediately to make sure I didn't have PE (pulmonary embolism), a blockage in one or more arteries caused by blood clots. At the hospital, I was told I had congestive heart failure, and I was transported to another hospital for further observation and echocardiography. The test came back normal this time, and my doctors really never could pin point my problem. Knowing all I know now, I believe these complications were due to my having the trait.

After that scare, I thought I was done having kids, but in 2010, I was pregnant again. My third child, Rodney, has SC disease, the same thing my husband has. I came home from the hospital and all was fine until the night I started having a sickle cell pain crisis in both my arms and both legs, excruciating pain like I had never experienced before in my life. We tried heating pads and hot baths, which helped, but as soon as I was out of the bath tub or off the heating pad, I was back at level 10 pain. I decided to go to the hospital that night, and the staff started giving me pain medication. By 1:00 the next afternoon, I told my nurse that I had a camera interview at my house at 4:00 pm with Discovery Studios and needed to be released. As soon as we pulled up to my house, I got out of the car and I could barely walk, with the pain the same magnitude it had been at the hospital. When the filming ended, I was driven right back to the hospital, and the next day I was in ICU. I was having a sickle cell pain crisis in both legs and arms; I also had congestive heart failure, fluid around my heart, high blood pressure, a lung infection, pneumonia, I was on oxygen because I was having a hard time breathing, and I had to have a blood transfusion because I had lost a lot of blood as this was just one or two weeks after I delivered my third child. Again, having the trait and being pregnant proved for me to be a dangerous combination. I knew in my heart the true cause of my suffering. Two weeks later, I was able to come home. Looking back at the video tapes my husband made of me while in the hospital, and just knowing all that happened to me, I realize now I was so close to death. But I also believe the Lord had a different plan for me.

In 2012, I experienced another crisis. I was working out daily and wasn't drinking enough water. My body was dehydrated, and a few days later I was in so much pain, my left arm was hurting so much, that I knew I had to go to the doctor. At the time, I thought I pulled a muscle, but later found out I was having a crisis from being dehydrated. As a child, I remember my brother and I always suffered from arm or leg pains but we just suffered through it. We never went to the doctor for it, we just cried ourselves to sleep many nights. Now I understand that we were experiencing pain crisis. When people say, "I have the trait and I never experience crisis," that may be true for some, but there has been pro athletes who has died from the trait. I have the trait and I didn't experience my first major crisis until I was 35 years old. I was near death when it happened, and then again at age 38. People with the trait must be vigilant in noticing any unexplained pains they may be experiencing. It could be sickle cell-related.

Psalm 41:3

[3] The Lord will sustain him on his sickbed and restore him from his bed of illness.

Chapter 2

Aiden's Battle Begins

Starting life with my sickle cell baby was marked by so much confusion and heavy emotions. I was hurt and couldn't focus. Every time he would get a fever, I would automatically think "he is having a crisis" because fevers with SS disease can lead to a sickle cell crisis. On our first visit to the hospital, I brought a stack of papers and endless questions for the doctor. I had done so much research and I was trying to figure out how his doctors could minimize my baby's crisis without having to worry about horrible side effects. I left the hospital that day feeling more lost and discouraged than when I arrived. My baby was only three months old. His doctor told me I shouldn't see any problems the first six months of life, because he still had fetal hemoglobin, but I knew that after six months, sickle cell babies start to lose their fetal hemoglobin.

My son had his first crisis at age one. He began to have acute splenic sequestration. It was explained to me that when sickled cells block the blood vessels leading out of the spleen, blood stays in the spleen instead of flowing through it, causing the spleen to get bigger. When this happens the blood count (hemoglobin and hematocrit) falls and the spleen gets very large and easy to feel. This is called splenic sequestration crisis (or "spleen crisis") which can be painful. I was further told that after age five, my son's spleen would likely shrink up and die and he wouldn't have any more spleen crises thereafter.

This episode was the first of numerous of trips to the emergency room in 2009. Aiden was in the hospital every three months with a spleen crisis. His hospital stays would range from one to two weeks each time. He wasn't making any red blood cells and his hemoglobin was always considerably low. When the hemoglobin continues to drop this can be fatal, and so his doctor suggested a blood transfusion. This was another blow to me: my one-year-old baby needed a blood transfusion. I knew we had to do it so we did, and everything went well with it. By the end of 2009, Aiden was admitted to the hospital for the third time that year needing another blood transfusion. At this point, I turned to my husband and said, "I cannot do this anymore." I had no idea what I was going to do, but I knew I was going to do something different. I

10

refused to let my child live his entire life in a hospital. I was determined not to let this disease stop me and my family from enjoying life. Aiden's doctors had told me about hydroxyurea and how it helps minimize sickle cell crisis by producing more red blood cells to prevent crisis from coming on. I was really desperate, so I said I would think about it, talk to my husband and do more research. I read all the positive research about it but once I started reading the side effects I quickly changed my mind. That drug was not an option for us anymore. And suddenly I knew: this was it. The medical profession could not do any more for my child; they could not do any more to help minimize these crises.

Even before Aiden was born, we saved our daughter's stem cells so that if we had a child with sickle cell disease we could do a stem cell transplant. Stem cells are the building blocks of the body, and have the ability to create our organs, blood tissue, and the immune system. Stem cells can be found in places like bone marrow and fat tissue, but the youngest, most flexible stem cells in the body come from the umbilical cord. When Mariah was born, my gynecologist, Dr. Tania White Jackson, informed us that this would be a great idea since there was a strong possibility of having a baby with sickle cell disease, so with extensive research and taking my doctor's advice, we decided to keep Mariah's stem cells. Dr. Jackson gave us literature on a company called CBR (Cord Blood Registry). Cord blood banking means collecting and storing the blood from within the umbilical cord (the part of the placenta that delivers nutrients to a fetus) after a baby is born. Cord blood contains blood-forming stem cells which are potentially useful for treating diseases that require stem cells transplants, also called bone marrow transplants, such as certain kinds of leukemia or lymphoma, severe sickle cell disease and severe combined immunodeficiency. After Mariah's delivery, Dr. Jackson arranged to collect her stem cells and sent them off to CBR. In doing so, my daughter's healthy cells, which have the trait, would be available to replace my son's. After a stem cell transplant procedure, Aiden would not have sickle cell disease anymore and would have just the trait like his sister. Because Aiden was having so many crises, one after the other, my husband and I discussed this option with my son's hematologist, who told us that our son may or may not be a match, that this procedure is long and drawn out, and that they do these procedures only on people with very severe cases of the disease. From my own research, I also knew that sometimes the procedure doesn't "take" and sometimes it is fatal. Did I want to put my son through this excruciating procedure? And what if it wasn't successful? What if it produced the very worst outcome imaginable?

Feeling completely without options, I turned to herbs. I had been studying herbs for about seven years by this time. I believed in the power of herbs ever since my mom told me that when she was a little girl growing up in the 1940s and 1950s, she never went to the hospital, and barely needed to see a doctor for anything. Her grandmother cured every sickness she had with a plant or some kind of tea. Finally, I knew what I had to do. This was my motivation to start treating my son's sickle cell disease with herbs.

Chapter 3

What Is Sickle Cell Disease?

Sickle cell disease is a disorder that affects the red blood cells, which use a protein called hemoglobin to transport oxygen from the lungs to the rest of the body. Normally, red blood cells are round and flexible so they can travel freely through the narrow blood vessels. Sickle cells are half-moon shaped, and it's difficult for abnormally shaped cells to pass through blood vessels. Unlike normal red blood cells, which can live for 120 days, sickle-shaped cells live only ten to twenty days. People with sickle cell disease have a mutation in a gene on chromosome 11, and as a result, hemoglobin molecules don't form properly, causing red blood cells to be rigid and have an abnormal shape. These irregularly shaped cells get stuck in the blood vessels and are unable to transport oxygen effectively, causing pain and damage to the organs.

Sickle cell anemia can lead to a host of complications, including:

Stroke. A stroke can occur if sickle cells block blood flow to an area of the brain. Signs of stroke include seizures, weakness or numbness of the arms and legs, sudden speech difficulties, and loss of consciousness. If a baby or child has any of these signs and symptoms, seek medical treatment immediately. A stroke can be fatal.

Acute chest syndrome. This life-threatening complication of sickle cell anemia causes chest pain, fever and difficulty breathing. Acute chest syndrome can be caused by a lunch infection or by sickle cells blocking blood vessels in the lungs. It may require emergency medical treatment with antibiotics and other treatments.

Pulmonary hypertension. People with sickle cell anemia can also develop high blood pressure in their lungs, or pulmonary hypertension. Shortness of breath and difficulty breathing are common symptoms of this condition, which can be fatal.

Organ damage. When sickle cells block blood flow through blood vessels, organs are immediately deprived of blood and oxygen. In sickle cell anemia, blood is also chronically low on oxygen. Chronic deprivation of oxygen-rich blood can damage nerves and organs in the body, including kidneys, liver and spleen. Organ damage can be fatal.

Blindness. Tiny blood vessels that supply the eyes can get blocked by sickle cells. Over time, this can damage the retina, the part of the eye that processes visual images, and lead to blindness.

Skin ulcers. Sickle cell anemia can cause open sores, called ulcers, on legs.

Gallstones. The breakdown of red blood cells produces a substance called bilirubin. A high level of bilirubin in the body can lead to gallstones.

Priapism. Men with sickle cell anemia may experience painful, long-lasting erections, a condition called priapism. As occurs in other parts of the body, sickle cells can block the blood vessels in the penis. This can damage the penis and eventually lead to impotence.

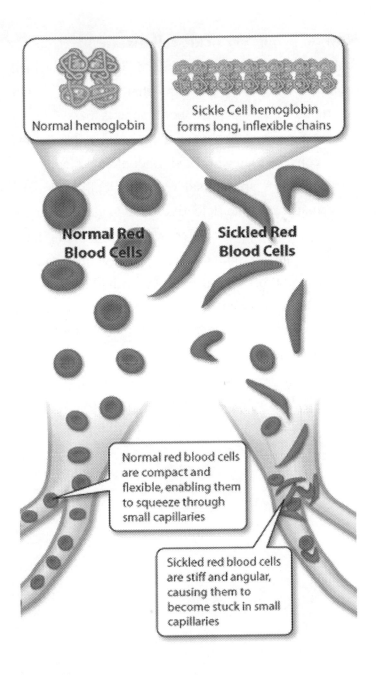

How do people get sickle cell disease?

Sickle cell disease is inherited in an autosomal recessive pattern. This means that a child will not inherit the disease unless both parents pass down a defective copy of the gene. People who inherit one good copy of the gene and one mutated copy are carriers. They are considered "clinically normal," but can still pass the defective gene to their children. Although they are carriers, they can still have serious problems and this is critically important to understand. Professional athletes with the trait have died from it. Dehydration, low oxygen levels, muscle fatigue, extreme heat and high altitude can all cause serious problems.

Sickle cell is inherited from two parents who are carriers, meaning both parents have the trait.

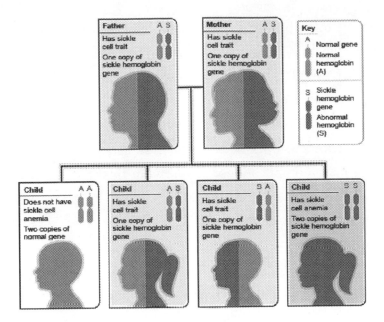

What are the symptoms of sickle cell disease?

Sickle cell disease prevents oxygen from reaching the spleen, liver, kidneys, lungs, heart, and other organs, causing significant damage. Without oxygen, the cells that make up these organs will begin to die. For example, the spleen is often destroyed in these patients, resulting in some loss of immune function. As a result, these patients often experience frequent infections. The red blood cells of patients with sickle cell disease don't live as long as healthy red blood cells. As a result, people with the disorder often have low red blood cell counts, or anemia, which is why this disease is commonly referred to as sickle cell anemia. When sickle-shaped red blood cells get stuck in blood vessels, this can cause episodes of pain called crises. Other symptoms include delayed growth, strokes, and jaundice, a yellowish hue to the skin and eyes because of liver damage. Because of these complications, people with this disorder are likely to have their life span reduced by about 30 years. The average person with full-blown sickle cell disease lives to be 40 years of age.

Who gets sickle cell disease?

In the United States, the disease most commonly affects African-Americans. Approximately one of every 500 African-American babies born in the United States has sickle cell anemia. It is most prevalent among people from Africa, India, the Caribbean, the Middle East, and the Mediterranean.

How is sickle cell disease diagnosed?

Most states routinely screen newborns for sickle cell disease with a simple blood test. If the disorder is not detected at birth, a blood sample can be used in a test called hemoglobin electrophoresis. This test will determine whether a person has sickle cell disease, or whether he or she is a carrier of the faulty hemoglobin gene.

How is sickle cell disease typically treated?

Babies and young children with sickle cell disease typically take a daily dose of penicillin to prevent potentially deadly infections, and folic acid, which helps build new red blood cells. Doctors advise people with sickle cell disease to get plenty of rest, drink lots of water, and avoid too much physical activity. Blood transfusions that provide healthy red blood cells are a common treatment. People with more severe cases of the disease can be treated with a bone marrow transplant. This procedure provides healthy red blood cells from a donor, ideally from a sibling.

There is currently no cure for sickle cell disease, although medical researchers are working on a cure and my son should see a cure in his lifetime. But for right now, the only way to manage SS disease is to eat a healthy diet full of fruits and vegetables, avoid strenuous exercise, manage stress, don't let your body temperature get too cold and drink plenty of water. And while every doctor will tell you to do these things, none of this was enough for my son. We followed every bit of this advice, but his crises still happened. For me and my family, we had to look deeper and find our own solutions.

Philippians 4:13

I can do all things through Christ which strengthens me.

Chapter 4

The Healers

On this journey I have had the pleasure of meeting and getting to know two amazing doctors who share my passion for herbs. I have learned a great deal about herbs from these healers, and have started incorporating many of them in my son's regimen. Their lists of herbs here, combined with those I discovered on my own, are what I have used to help my son win the sickle cell battle.

Dr. Charlie Ware, AP, LLC, Acupuncturist

Dr. Ware studied at the Pacific College of Oriental Medicine, San Diego CA and the Atlantic Institute of Oriental Medicine, Fort Lauderdale, Florida. He holds a bachelor's degree in philosophy and biological sciences from the University of Maryland. After graduating, Dr. Ware traveled extensively, studying acupuncture, herbs and homeopathic medicine. It was during these travels that Dr. Ware was exposed to a multitude of illnesses and conditions that traditional medicine found difficult or impossible to treat. Dr. Ware treats a host of conditions but specializes in infertility, gastrointestinal disorders, hormone replacement therapy, neuromuscular disorders, low back pain, shoulder pain, homeopathy, and weight loss and pain management. He practices in Hollywood, Florida.

Dr. Nagaratina Salem, M.D.

Dr. Nagaratina Salem is my children's pediatrician. She received her medical degree from Kilpauk Medical College, Chennai, India in 1993. Dr. Salem completed her first two years of pediatric residency in New York, and her third year at University of Texas HSC, El Paso, where she received her "Resident of the Year" award. Later, Dr. Salem practiced in Athens, Texas, providing comprehensive pediatric care, and moved to Plano in 2001. She worked as a locum physician, gaining diverse experiences in many practices across the Dallas-Fort Worth area before establishing her own practice, "Kiddie Docs," in 2004. Dr. Salem is board certified by the American Board of Pediatrics and has completed her MBA in Healthcare Management from University of Texas at Dallas. She now practices at Craig Ranch Pediatrics in McKinney, Texas.

Dr. Ware has compiled the following information and recommendations:

In traditional herbal medicine, herbs are used in various combinations in order to truly heal the patient. It is very rare to use only a single herb to treat a patient. If this is done, it is only for a short time to elicit a particular response. Once that response is reached, either a compound formula is administered and the single herb is included in the formula or stopped all together. Although the following provides comprehensive information about each herb, it is still best to be treated by a professional herbalist, acupuncturist, naturopathic physician or nutriceutical specialist in your area. Although herbs are natural, they still are considered medicine and can be harmful if not taken properly.

Sickle cell disease has unique properties and mechanisms of action in how it presents itself in patients. There are four herbal categories for treatment according to their phytochemical and biomedical components. These categories are: Blood invigorating and pain relieving, oxygen supporting and oxidation reducing, anti-inflammatory, and antibacterial/antiviral. These are the four most important aspects of any medicine or herb in treating SCD. Each patient should consult a qualified health practitioner before beginning herbal compounds.

Each of the categories used to classify the herbs discussed in this section plays a role in the treatment of sickle cell disease due to their unique characteristics. Blood invigorating and pain relieving herbs have the unique ability to move blood in the vessels rather quickly. The importance of this action is that in patients with SCD, the red blood cells become stuck together or the blood's viscosity is too thick, causing pain. Even worse, organ or tissue necrosis can ensue. These herbs have the property of vasodilatation. By giving the blood more room to move, the congealed blood has the ability to exit the pain area, leaving room for fresh, nutrient rich blood to enter. Another key property of these herbs is that they are energy boosters and cardio protectors. This essentially means that, when taken properly, each herb in this category will combat fatigue without raising blood pressure or damaging cardiac tissue, unlike energy drinks or various enzymes or herbs used incorrectly to get the false boost of energy that creates a host of other health problems.

Oxygen supporting and oxidation reducing herbs have the properties that have been shown to either allow the body to efficiently use its oxygen or aid in the process to produce oxygen. Herbs in this category contain phytochemicals that through research have proven to be powerful antioxidants. The lack of oxygen in a SCD patient is critical to energy production, organ tissue health and blood ph levels.

Anti-inflammation herbs have properties that rid the body of inflammation in several ways. The first way is to quickly move blood to the local area depending on the direct cause of inflammation, i.e. injury or allergic reactions. Another pathway for the phytochemicals in the herbs to help reduce inflammation is to directly affect cellular processes that create inflammation. These herbs have been shown to effect interleukins, histamine and mast cells, all cellular components that propagate inflammation.

Antibiotic/antiviral herbs all display properties that decrease rogue bacteria and viruses in the body, but they won't strip the body of its good bacteria. Herbs in this category also have antiviral components that help increase killer T-cells, lymphocytes and interferons. By using herbs with these cellular components, the body is able to combat harmful bacteria and viruses, giving us what we know as immunity. The use of these herbs will cut the need for prescription antibiotics which are harsh and strip the body of all bacteria, good and bad.

It must be noted that the herbs are listed here by their primary biomedical function, but some of the herbs will have cross-category properties that will be listed as well.

Blood invigorating/pain relieving herbs:

Chuan Xiong's properties include cardiogenic, microcirculation, immune booster, analgesic and anticoagulant. The important phytochemical in Chuan Xiong is tetramethylpyrazine, which has been shown to increase blood circulation in cardiac disease and treat headaches. Another phytochemical of Chuan Xiong is ligustrazine. This has been proven to protect neurons and increase microcirculation of venioles in the brain and peripheral areas of the body. The most important action is that it acts as a cardiac vasodilator and peripheral blood flow booster. Chuan Xiong also inhibits red blood cells from sticking together, preventing thrombus. Chuan Xiong has immune properties as well. It has been shown to increase natural killer cells, lymphocytes and phagocyes. Clinically, Chuan Xiong is used to treat pain associated with poor circulation of blood. It has also been used to treat swelling from trauma and to promote healing time from surgery and injuries. With Chuan Xiong's microcirculation properties it is used to increase blood flow to organs to prevent ischemia and lower blood pressure.

Dan Shen, or salvia, improves blood circulation and vasodilation, has anti-inflammatory properties, and is cardiogenic. Tanshinone is the active phytochemical in Dan Shen that has been shown to inhibit platelet aggregation, dilate blood vessels and reduce fever and inflammation. Research has proven its microcirculation properties help with angina and liver function as well. Dan Shen revitalizes the blood by increasing oxygen and viscosity of the blood. Its ability to decrease fevers and inflammation makes it a very common herb to use for flu and cold season. The vasodilatation properties of Dan Shen help to cool the blood and reduce inflammation and fevers.

Dong Quai is a blood builder, antispasmodic, vasodilator, and anticoagulator. Dong Quai contains vitamins E and A, and is one of the few herbs that contains vitamin B12. The active phytochemicals are coumarins and ferulic acid. Coumarin has been shown to be a major vasodilator and antispasmodic.

In addition, it has a stimulating effect on the central nervous system where it relaxes peripheral smooth muscles. Ferulic acid prevents spasming, reduces blood clotting and relaxes peripheral blood vessels.

Black cohosh is antispasmodic, analgesic, and increases microcirculation. Isoferulic acid and salicylic acid are present and have effects on the musculoskeletal system and in anti-inflammation. Salicylic acid has been shown to have a profound effect on the lower body. It has been used to treat lower gastric and uterine spasming and increasing microcirculation. Black cohosh extract and homeopathics have been used post-operatively to heal tissue because of their microcirculation properties.

Atractylodes rhizome is analgesic, anti-inflammatory, anti-ulcer, anticoagulating, and effects smooth muscles. Its main phytochemicals are atractylenolide and beta-eudesmol. Both have a profound effect on the stomach to decrease pain from spasming and protect the stomach lining. Atractylenolide increases gastric capillary permeability, thus increasing blood flow. This process will decrease spasming and cramping of the intestine. Beta-eudesmol decreases acid in the stomach but also has a micro-circulation effect in peripheral capillaries, thus decreasing the risk of ischemia and ulcers in various parts of the body.

Oxygen supporting/ oxidation resistant herbs:

Ginkgo biloba increases oxygen, increases memory, protects the cardiovascular system and has antioxidant properties. Its main phytochemicals are ginkgolides and flavonoids. Ginkgolides has been shown to treat arterial insufficiency in the lower limbs and brain, which can improve glucose utilization in the brain, thus improving alertness of alpha wave rhythms. It has further been shown to improve eyesight by affecting the oxygen free radicals in and around the eyes.

Hawthorne is a powerful antioxidant, cardiac protector, anti-inflammatory, and atherosclerosis inhibitor. Hawthorne's main phytochemicals are glycosides and phelonic compounds. Glycosides have been shown to increase blood oxygen levels and increase cardiac output. Glycosides have proven to reduce the number of free radicals in the blood, but even more important, in and around the heart. This same chemical has been shown to inhibit interleukins, inflammatory active cells.

Cordyceps is an antioxidant, benefits the vascular system, enhances cellular oxygen uptake, builds muscle and has anti-aging and anti-fatigue properties. The phytochemicals of cordyceps are mannitol and cordycepin. The presence of these two chemicals has shown to increase ATP of the muscle cells, essentially increasing the functional output of each cell. Additionally, and more importantly, this increases the level of oxygen in the blood. This improves blood function, kills free radicals, decreases stress on the heart, builds muscle and improves tissue repair.

Ginseng treats exhaustion, increases mental performance and improves the immune system. The active phytochemical in ginseng, Eleuthero, is an adaptogen, which helps the body resist many forms of stress. Eleuthero helps recharge the adrenal glands and increase oxygen permeability of the cells. Adrenal function has been associated with greater immune response and physical and energy increase. This chemical has also been shown to increase killer T-cells which destroy viruses and cancers.

Anti-inflammation herbs:
Bupleurum is anti-inflammatory and a liver cleanser. Saikosaponins and saikosides are the active

phytochemicals in bupleirum. Saikosaponins have been shown to be anti-inflammatory by increasing cytokines, immune response chemicals. This production of cytokines does not to appear to be disease-specific. Saikosides protect the liver from toxicity and improves liver function. It has been shown to continually eliminate impurities and waste matter from the system.

Licorice root is anti-spasmodic, increases levels of interferon, has anti-viral and anti-bacterial qualities. Glycyrrhizin is the active phytochemical in licorice root that affects the adrenal glands to produce cortisol. Cortisol is the body's natural corticosteroid, aiding with inflammation and pain throughout the body. Glycyrrhizin also inhibits prostaglandins, another inflammation response chemical. This same chemical has an effect on interferon production as well. By increasing interferon production the herb has an antiviral effect.

Pulsatilla is anti-inflammatory, anti-infection, antispasmodic and analgesic. Anemonin is the chief phytochemical that has a profound effect on gastric muscle and tissue. By effecting the microcirculation and capillaries, the gastric spasm and inflammation is reduced, also relieving pain. The chemical has also shown to increase macrophage activity thus increasing killer T-cells and effecting infections in various parts of the body.

Antiviral and antibacterial herbs:

Astragalus is antiviral, antioxidant and increases immunity. Asparagines have been identified as one of the phytochemicals to stimulate the immune system. One clinical trial indicated that asparagines have been shown to boost T-cell levels and white blood cells, which can prevent influenza and the common cold. Astragalus has phytochemicals that increase microcirculation in peripheral, coronary, cerebral and intestinal vessels. These properties help to reduce blood pressure and the development of mature blood cells.

Echinacea is antiviral, antioxidant, anti-inflammatory and an immune booster. Purified polysaccharide and alkylamide have been identified as phytochemicals to increase lymphocytes, phagocytosis stimulation, macrophages activating and antigen-specific immune responses. These have activity to inhibit edema, COX I and COX II enzymes secretions which have been shown to inhibit rhinovirus. Anti-inflammation phytochemicals that mediate nitric oxide are echinacea spp and E. sanguine. Echinacea spp scavenges free radicals and suppresses low density lipoproteins oxidation. **NOTE: Echinacea should not be taken for long periods of time. Take for only two to five weeks and discontinue for three to four weeks.**

Wolfberry improves immunity, nourishes blood and is antioxidant. Lycium barbarium polysaccharide has been identified as the primary phytochemical that has a duel effect to boost the immune system by cleaning the hydroxygen free radicals, lymphocytes and T-cell production. Wolfberry nourishes blood because it contains 19 different amino acids and vitamins and 21 minerals. It also has a higher content of beta carotene than carrots and a protein effect greater than bee pollen.

Golden seal is antibiotic, antiviral and analgesic. The alkaloid berberine gives golden seal immunity properties. Golden seal has been used to treat infectious diarrhea, upper respiratory tract infections and digestive mucous membrane disorders. Berberine has been shown to kill various germs, yeast, viruses and parasites. White blood cells are activated by berberine so this can explain its antibiotic and disinfectant function. **NOTE: Golden seal should be taken only for short periods of time (two to four weeks only) followed by rest for at least three to four weeks before it is resumed**.

There are two more herbs that should be part of the arsenal of anyone with sickle cell disease. Dr. Salem has compiled the following information and recommendations here:

The **neem** tree has been growing in India for the more than 2,000 years. The medicinal properties of neem have been known for centuries. It is very good for purifying the blood as it is toxic to bacterial as well as viral organisms. It is also used against worm infestation and as a mosquito repellent due to its pungent odor. It is very helpful to cleanse the blood of any diseases and keep a person healthy. In sickle cell disease, the decrease in the patient's immunity would increase their potential to get sick. Using a small amount of neem as a powder would be useful to ward off infections.

Turmeric is the root of an herbaceous plant which belongs to the ginger family. This has traditionally been used in Indian cooking due to its antiseptic properties. It also contains high levels of salicylic acid which helps to thin the blood and decrease the chances of blood clots and sickle cell crisis. It is available as a powder and can be added to most dishes while cooking.

It is important to note that, although many of these herbs can be used alone, the maximum benefit is in combination with other herbs creating a compound. Although there are many healing herbs and plants on this earth, I have chosen only a few that have helped with my son's sickle cell disease. Since he started taking these herbs, Aiden is full of energy and living a very healthy and full life.

Genesis 1:29
[29] Then God said, "I give you every seed-bearing plant on the face of the whole earth and every tree that has fruit with seed in it. They will be yours for food.

Chapter 5

More Miracle Herbs

When Aiden was only six months old, I asked his doctor, "If I could find something that would raise my son's hemoglobin, something that would build new red blood cells, improve blood circulation and increase his oxygen, would I be on the right track to reducing his crises?" The doctor answered yes, and that was the last time I depended on Aiden's medical doctors to help me minimize his sickle cell crises.

I remembered talking with my dear friend, Stacey Ward years earlier about liquid chlorophyll. I had no idea what it was, but she explained it was great for anemia. Three years later, when I recalled that conversation, I started researching liquid chlorophyll. Once I realized its benefits, I quickly purchased some and started giving it to my son. All the leafy green vegetables contain chlorophyll. When we eat spinach, kale, cabbage, and collard greens, we are eating chlorophyll. I also learned at the time that any time we cook our food too long, as southerners tend to do with vegetables, we quickly cook the nutrients and chlorophyll right out. Chlorophyll is called the blood of plants. It collects light and uses the light to make energy in plants. Chlorophyll is the compound that gives plants their green color. It heals, cleanses, and destroys many harmful bacteria and cancer cells. It is as important as sunlight: without it, life would not be possible. In fact, hemoglobin and chlorophyll have similar structures. The primary function of hemoglobin is to transport oxygen from the lungs to other parts of the body. Hemoglobin is composed of four elements: carbon, hydrogen, oxygen and nitrogen. All four are organized around iron. Chlorophyll is composed of the same elements, which are organized around magnesium.

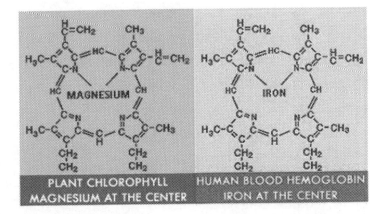

In sickle cell anemia, the abnormal hemoglobin (Hemoglobin S) sticks together when it gives up its oxygen to the tissues. These clumps cause red blood cells to become stiff and shaped like a sickle. Chlorophyll helps do the job of hemoglobin when ingested. It promotes healthy circulation, cleanses the body, increases the number of red blood cells and therefore increases oxygen throughout the body. In other words, chlorophyll helps build hemoglobin. This is exactly what our sickle cell babies and others need.

Want more evidence? Liquid chlorophyll also reduces excess cholesterol and fatty acids, promotes normal brain development, activates liver cells and eliminates and neutralizes toxins. And that's not all. It also enhances intelligence and memory, stimulates heartbeat, improves the digestive system, and, most critically, raises hemoglobin. Where sickle cells cause oxygen deprivation, bad blood circulation and low hemoglobin, liquid chlorophyll's benefits counter every one of these detriments, naturally.

Eight months after I introduced my son to liquid chlorophyll, he had a pain crisis in his leg. This is when I did more research and realized you need more than one herb to fight sickle cell anemia. Chlorophyll is wonderful but I needed something else to work in conjunction with it. I knew that his blood was clotting together and forming abnormal sickle cells which couldn't pass through his blood vessels, causing the pain. That's when I discovered nattokinase-serrapeptase. Nattokinase, or natto extract, is the enzyme that is extracted from natto, a traditional Japanese food made from fermented soybeans that has been consumed in Japan for years. It contains large amounts of fibrinolytic activity, a process that prevents blood clots from growing and becoming problematic. It purifies the blood and gets rid of all the bad protein and toxins in the blood and causes the blood to flow in its natural state. I chose this herb because one of its major functions is to keep the blood flowing and not clotting and sticking together. Serrapeptase, only just discovered in the early 1970s, is an enzyme located in the intestines of silkworms. It is a superior enzyme that provides anti-inflammatory properties and has the ability to break down non-living tissue in the body. It also has been shown to act as an anti-inflammatory and a pain blocker, and may help with plaque build-up in arteries. I learned about nattokinase-serrapeptase from a wonderful man who worked at a natural health store in my city. Tom was once a medical doctor, but he gave it up, traveled the world and studied natural herbs and healings, and that became his life. He left the medical field and started helping people with the knowledge he learned through traveling the world and studying different plants and herbs. At his recommendation, I immediately started Aiden on nattokinase-serrapeptase.

Benefits of Nattokinase

Promotes blood circulation

Regulates cholesterol

Improves bone density and reduces pain in the muscles and joints

Regulates blood pressure

Prevents strokes and heart disease

Prevents osteoporosis

During this period, I came to learn about colostrum and its benefit to those fighting sickle cell disease. Colostrum is the thin yellowish fluid produced during the first few milkings of a mammal after she has given birth. It is the carrier of the immunities that are transferred from mother to infant, and one of the reasons breast feeding is so important to the health of babies. Colostrum contains an abundance of nutrients, including growth factors, lipidic and glucidic factors, oligosaccharides, antimicrobials, cytokines and nucleoside. It is rich in immunoglobulins, which are certain types of protein involved in promoting the immune system and fighting germs. You can get raw colostrum from your local dairy farmer. It needs to be refrigerated and consumed within a reasonably short time. Raw colostrum differs from processed colostrum because its immune factors come from just one cow, whereas processed colostrum comes from a pool of hundreds or thousands of cows and provides a broad spectrum of immune factors. Choose colostrum from pasture-fed cows. They have a higher range of immunities. Be sure your colostrum comes from animals that are pesticide, antibiotic and rBST free, and is processed with very low heat. The compression used to create colostrum tablets will cause the colostrum to be exposed to excessive heat, so buy colostrum only in powdered form or in capsules.

Another super food I learned about, beet root juice also helps raise hemoglobin and contains many wonderful nutritional compounds such as magnesium, phosphorus, potassium, calcium, copper, selenium, zinc, iron and manganese. It contains amino acids, antioxidants, vitamins A, B1, B2, B3, C and folic acid. Beet root juice protects against precancerous esophageal lesions and tumors. It's an anti-inflammatory, improves digestion, and helps create healthy red blood cells and maximize the amount of oxygen being carried.

I first heard of moringa, "the miracle plant," from one of my followers on my blog, a woman who lives in Tanzania. Moringa oleifera contains more than 92 nutrients and 46 types of antioxidants. Moringa is said to cure hundreds of diseases and has almost every vitamin found in fruits and vegetables, only in larger proportions. Moringa is considered a complete food as it contains all of the essential amino acids required for a healthy body. The dried leaf is a nutritional powerhouse and contains all essential as well as non-essential amino acids. With all the health benefits of this miracle herb, it can easily be considered the most nutritious herb on earth. There are no side-effects and it can be consumed by small children as well as adults. Today, millions of people the world over have started using moringa-based products in porridge, pastas and bread to reap the health benefits of the extraordinary moringa herb.

Moringa: a nutritional powerhouse
- 92 nutrients
- 46 antioxidants
- 36 anti-inflammatories
- 18 amino acids, 9 essential amino acids
- Nourishes the immune system
- Promotes healthy circulation
- Supports normal glucose levels
- Natural anti-aging benefits
- Promotes healthy digestion
- Promotes heightened mental clarity
- Boosts energy without caffeine
- Encourages balanced metabolism
- Promotes softer skin
- Provides relief from acne
- Supports normal hormone levels

Examples of the nutritional value of moringa
(gram-for-gram comparison of nutritional data)

2 times **the protein of yogurt**
3 times **the potassium of bananas**
4 times **the calcium of milk**
4 times **the vitamin A of carrots**
7 times **the vitamin C of oranges**

Soon after being introduced to moringa, I discovered Dong Quai and astragalus. Aiden's school called and said that he had been complaining about pain in his legs and arms all day. I instantly called Dr. Ware and asked what I could give my son to help him get over the crisis fast. He told me to go to the store and purchase these items, and so I did. When I arrived home, my son was playing, so I didn't have to use the Dong Quai or astragalus that particular day. Two months later, however, Aiden told me his hands were beginning to hurt. I immediately gave him the Dong Quai and astragalus I had picked up for him, and continued administering them three times daily for the next three days. A pain crisis never manifested. I always have Dong Quai and astragalus on hand now and I use these two myself if I think I may be starting to have a pain crisis. Because I've experienced sickle cell pain crises before, I know the signs. The pain always starts off as minor aches in my hands, arms or legs, but within an hour or so, that minor pain can quickly spike to level 10 pain.

Genesis 1:12

[12] And the earth brought forth grass and herb yielding seed after his kind, and the tree yielding fruit, whose seed was in itself, after his kind: and God saw that it was good.

Chapter 6

Aiden's Last Crisis

Aiden had a crisis over the holidays in 2012, a very difficult and exhausting week. We went out of town and I ran out of chlorophyll. I don't know what I was thinking but I decided to buy the chlorophyll once we arrived back home, thinking he would be fine going five days without taking his herbs. Aiden had a crisis on the fifth day—the pain started in his hands and gradually moved to his arms. We drove back home to get pain medication, and I immediately started him back on liquid chlorophyll, nattokinase-serrapeptase, vitamins B6, folic acid, B12 and D3. After two days I noticed his left elbow was swollen so I took him to the hospital because I had never seen this before. They did the standard CBC, culture, fluids, antibiotics and x-ray on his arm.

Amazingly, his hemoglobin was good and he was making plenty of new red blood cells. All his numbers and counts were in great standing according to his doctor. (In the past, before I started the herbs, his numbers were always low and he was never making red blood cells.) The very next day his hemoglobin dropped to 6.8 from 8. It dropped just that quick, of course, because I didn't take his herbs to the hospital with us. I was so anxious to get him out of there so I could start him back on his herbs. If his hemoglobin were to drop down to 6, I knew they would have to give him another blood transfusion. The next day, his arm was swollen from his elbow down to his wrist, and it was hard and hot. His hemoglobin was still 6.8, so he didn't need to have a blood transfusion. Initially we were told the swelling was a sickle cell bone infarct, which is the death of the bone. Bone infarct is an area of the bone tissue that has become necrotic as a result of loss of its arterial blood supply; then swelling sets in and it has to heal on its own, which can take weeks. Aiden's x-rays showed no sign of a bone infarct, and his medical team was stumped. They said it could be a bone infarct or an infection, but at that point they just didn't know for sure. I felt very frustrated that they couldn't explain the swelling, and I was concerned about a blood clot, but I was assured it wasn't that.

Aiden was released with a follow up appointment in four days. I went to see my healer friend Tom at the health food store to get his advice because I was feeling uneasy about the swelling. He advised me that Aiden's lymphatic system was being compromised. He showed me a picture of the lymphatic system and explained to me that it is an extensive drainage system that returns water and proteins from various tissues back to the bloodstream. It consists of a network of ducts, called lymph vessels. Some scientists consider this system to be part of the blood and circulatory systems because lymph comes from blood and returns to blood, and because its vessels are very similar to the veins and capillaries of the blood system. Throughout the body, wherever there are blood vessels, there are lymph vessels, and the two systems work together.

In sickle cell, when the blood becomes sickled shape and not able to pass through these vessels and lymph vessels, if there is no way for excess fluid to return to the blood, the body tissues become swollen. This may happen because there is too much fluid in the tissues in that area. The lymph vessels collect that excess fluid and carry it to the veins through the lymphatic system. This is what was going on with Aiden. Tom said to continue with natto and massage and the swelling would go down.

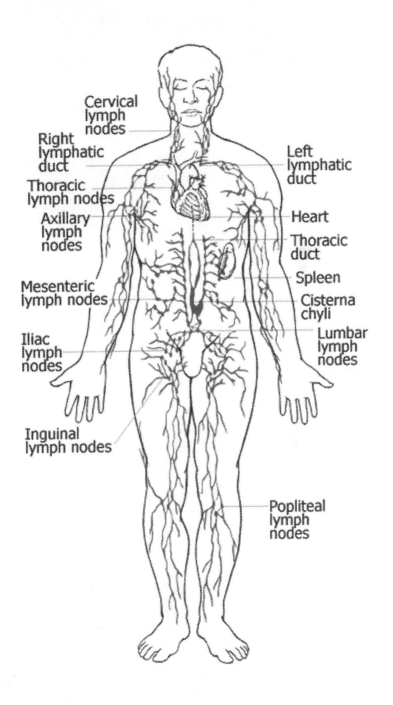

Cervical lymph nodes

Right lymphatic duct

Thoracic lymph nodes

Axillary lymph nodes

Mesenteric lymph nodes

Iliac lymph nodes

Inguinal lymph nodes

Left lymphatic duct

Heart

Thoracic duct

Spleen

Cisterna chyli

Lumbar lymph nodes

Popliteal lymph nodes

On my way home, I picked up beet juice powder, which also acts as an anti-inflammatory and raises hemoglobin. I gave Aiden daily baths with drops of tea tree and rosemary in the water. I massaged his hands and arms every few hours with rosemary and continued giving him liquid chlorophyll, natto, B vitamins, D3 and colostrum. A few days later, his arm was no longer swollen. I hated this had to happen. I'm thankful my son is on the road to recovery and I'm assured more than ever that the herbs are helping him in the most positive way. Before this happened, the last crisis he had had in his leg in 2010 lasted for two weeks. This time it lasted for five days, his arm was not swollen anymore and the pain was gone. I am certain that, if I wasn't giving my son these herbs, he would be one of the unfortunate ones who stays sick with crisis after crisis. I will not ever let him run out of herbs again. The Lord put everything on this earth that we need to sustain our health.

Aiden's regimen at four years of age:
Chlorophyll—20-30 drops twice daily

Nattokinase-serrapeptase—one pill four times per week

Moringa—one capsule four times per week

Beet root powder—One-half teaspoon in four ounces of 100% juice daily

Vitamin D3—5,000 IU daily

Dong Quai—One-half ML three times daily (I administer Dong Quai only if I notice Aiden is in the beginning stages of a crisis, when minor aches first start)

Astragalus—One-half ML three times daily (I give only at the sign of crisis)

Golden seal—One ML for five days. Because golden seal is a natural antibiotic, I do not administer this herb beyond five days, and give golden seal to my children only at the first sign of illness, if I notice a runny nose, low grade fever, coughing, or other cold-like symptoms.

Revelation 22:2

[2] down the middle of the great street of the city. On each side of the river stood the tree of life, bearing twelve crops of fruit, yielding its fruit every month. And the leaves of the tree are for the healing of the nations.

Chapter 7

Healthy Eating with Sickle Cell

Food plays a very important part in our lives. Eating processed food is dangerous for people without sickle cell, so anyone with sickle cell disease must be sure they are feeding their cells and tissues the best possible nutrition. All body cells need food to keep them healthy, and the type of foods eaten will determine how well the body tissues are able to work properly in order to prevent illness or keep a chronic illness from worsening. People with SS need lean meats, fish, lots of vegetables, fruits and whole grains in their diets. They need foods that have the highest nutritional value. Now, this doesn't mean never eating fast foods, but it does mean eating them in moderation. Everyday living for someone with sickle cell must center around healthy foods.

Because people with sickle cell disease are at greater risk of getting infection, it is important to handle food with particular care, for example, maintaining strict hand hygiene, storing foods properly and checking the expiration or 'use by' dates on food packaging including canned foods. It is also important to thoroughly defrost frozen food before cooking and to make sure chilled foods from the supermarket are cooked according to their instructions. Extra care needs to be taken when re-heating previously cooked food, making sure that the food is heated completely through, especially if using a microwave oven. Chicken and eggs are a common source of salmonella, so it is important to cook these and all foods thoroughly. Salmonella can lead to bone infection, which can be very difficult to treat in people with sickle cell disease.

Not eating for long periods can trigger a sickle cell crisis because there aren't any nutrients in the body to maintain normal bodily functions. With sickle cell disease, if fasting is part of an individual's religious practice, this should be discussed with a doctor or specialist nurse. Always seek advice on how to practice your religion without putting your health at risk.

In the past, I used to buy processed food, food with chemicals and preservatives and all sorts of harmful ingredients, with words I couldn't even pronounce, and I was putting these foods in my family's bodies. I had never really taken the time to study the ingredients in the food we ate, until one day, my husband bought pizza rolls and I decided to read the ingredients on the box. Some of these included sodium aluminum phosphate, chloride, preservatives, titanium dioxide, and sodium nitrate. I immediately trashed those pizza rolls, and have steered away from harmful food additives ever since. Why put anything in your body that doesn't have the highest possible nutritional value?

Other harmful ingredients to stay away from:

Artificial flavors. These chemicals come cheap and are used to mimic natural flavors of foods. They can cause allergic reactions, skin problems, asthma, and hyperactivity as well as affect your thyroid's function.

Artificial colors. These are chemicals taken from coal-tar derivatives that enhance the color of food. Like artificial flavors, they can cause headaches and fatigue, along with allergic reactions, skin problems and hyperactivity.

Artificial sweeteners. Also called Aspartame, these are found in sodas with zero calorie labels. You will end up thirstier and suffer a sugar crash that makes you crave more sugar. What's more, artificial sweeteners have been linked to cancer.

MSG (monosodium glutamate). Used as a flavor enhancer in many restaurant dishes, this appetite stimulator can cause headaches, weakness, difficulty in breathing and heartburn.

High fructose corn syrup. Cheaper than cane and beet sugar, and used in baked goods, it blends easily with any beverage. You can have a higher risk of obesity and Type 2 Diabetes with this food additive.

Hydrogenated or partially hydrogenated oils. From palm oils, vegetable oils to soybean oils, these are used in more than 40,000 food products in the United States. Hydrogenated oils have been found to increase your risk of getting arterial plaque that can cause heart disease.

These ingredients can be very damaging to our bodies in numerous ways. They can cause heart problems and nervous system problems, block the absorption of essential fatty acids, upset blood sugar regulation and more. When living healthy greatly depends on the foods we eat, it is so important to select healthy choices. Remember, if you can't pronounce the ingredient, chances are you do not need to put that item in your body.

Choosing Healthy Drinks

It is critically important to stay hydrated with sickle cell disease. Drink as much water as possible daily to prevent dehydration, one of the most common precursors of a pain crisis. There are so many unhealthy drinks everywhere you turn. The best drink options are coconut water, water, 100% juice, and juicing fresh vegetables and fruits. Stay away from sugary drinks, sodas, and artificial sweetener drinks.

Romans 8:28

And we know that all things God works for the good of those who love him, who have been called according to his purpose.

Chapter 8

The Immune and Digestive Systems

Another important factor to consider with sickle cell disease is our immune system. When school starts, I need to make sure my kids' immune systems are strong enough to fight off all the nasty germs and sickness they encounter at school. It's serious for a sickle cell child to get sick because they are prone to having crises. We want to make sure we give Aiden the best immune booster there is.

Colostrum is the first milk produced in mothers when breastfeeding. It is the first food of life. As I learned earlier, colostrum also produces large amounts of living cells which will defend against many harmful agents. It's naturally designed to maintain health and prevent diseases. Colostrum is incredibly effective at shutting down the cause of most diseases and infections. Colostrum was designed by nature to protect, activate, regulate, and support our immune systems. That's why colostrum is an important weapon in Aiden's arsenal.

Another great immune booster is golden seal, used for hundreds of years to treat and cure many illnesses. Golden seal's numerous uses are attributed to its antibiotic, anti-inflammatory and astringent properties. It soothes irritated mucus membranes, aiding the eyes, ears, nose and throat. Taken at the first signs of respiratory problems, colds or flu, golden seal can help to prevent further symptoms from developing. It has also been used to help reduce fevers and relieve congestion and excess mucous.

The Importance of the Digestive System

Everything starts in the gut. Most foods we eat are not in a form that the body can use as nourishment. Food and beverages must be changed into smaller molecules of nutrients before they can be absorbed into the blood and carried to cells throughout the body. So it's important to eat natural and healthy foods because, when broken down, their health-giving properties are going into your tissues and cells. When you put a lot of junk in your system such as processed food, food that contains preservatives, additives and chemicals, these toxins are going into your cells and tissues, which will cause problems. For those who eat their fair share of processed food, it's important to take a probiotic daily, because processed food removes the good bacteria in the body, whereas probiotics provide the body with a large quantity of the beneficial and good bacteria that's already found in the digestive tract. Probiotics are small organisms that help maintain the natural balance of other organisms in the digestive tract and intestines.

Vitamin D3 and Calcium for Sickle Cell Disease

There is a clinical trial taking place now studying whether oral vitamin D3 can decrease lung complications in children and adolescents with sickle cell disease. There are serious health issues for anyone who is deficient in D3. Forty percent of the U.S. population is vitamin D3-deficient. D3 protects against certain cancers, heart disease, strokes, bone fractures and a host of other problems. People think they get enough from the sun, but the truth is people with darker complexions such as African-Americans and those of Middle Eastern descent have melanin in the skin, reducing the amount of ultraviolet radiation entering the skin and protecting it from skin cancer. But the presence of melanin in the skin also blocks the amount of vitamin D3 we can get from the sun. It's a good idea to check your vitamin D levels when you go for a physical checkup.

The body needs vitamin D3 to absorb calcium, both of which play an important role in protecting bones. Without enough vitamin D, one can't produce enough of the hormone calcitrol (known as the "active vitamin D"). This in turn leads to insufficient calcium absorption from the diet, so the body must take calcium from its stores in the skeleton, weakening existing bone and preventing the formation of strong, new bone. Calcium and vitamin D work hand-in-hand together.

Psalm 22:19

God is our refuge and strength, an ever present help in trouble.

Chapter 9

My Vision for Aiden
and the Future of Sickle Cell

Since Aiden first started taking natural herbs, he has not had a sickle cell crisis, except for the one time I ran out of herbs and we were out of town. I have found the supplements that work for my son and keep him healthy, growing strong and free from pain. There are thousands of herbs growing all over the world that do so many wonderful things. We must find the right ones for our children and find what works best. I've had great success using a combination of herbs and vitamins as well as Dr. Charlie Ware's supplements. I have learned the importance of ensuring my son takes his supplements daily, and my vision for Aiden long-term is to get him in the habit of eating healthy and taking his supplements vigilantly. This is the most important thing he can learn and continue to do as he gets older and becomes an adult. I want him to understand how important it is to take care of his body, eat the right foods and never skip his daily supplements. I would like Aiden to be an example for all who suffer from this disease and to all the parents whose children suffer from sickle cell disease. Aiden is living proof that there is hope and healing for a better day and a better tomorrow. Our children are the future and we can learn, study and research how to help them live productive, healthy lives.

The future of sickle cell is going to be one great movement, and Dr. Charlie Ware is leading the way with his guidance, education and knowledge of sickle cell and many other diseases. Too many people are dying, hurting and suffering from this disease, and if we can bring relief to a few there will be millions more to follow. In Africa, there are millions of people suffering from sickle cell disease, and they have no medical help; they are in pain and the death rates are extremely high. Through connections, Dr. Ware was able to bring his herbs to Cameroon, Africa in July 2013 supported by Dr. Roger Tappa of Austin, Texas. Dr. Tappa is originally from Cameroon, and he has a passion and love for his country and wants to see improvement for sickle cell as well. The doctors in Cameroon are currently testing the herbs on severe cases of sickle cell and so far they are seeing improvement of sickle cell in his native country, and so far, they are seeing improvement and patients are feeling better after taking herbs for just three days.

If these trials prove to be successful, the goal is to get these herbs distributed throughout every part of Africa and bring relief and healing where it is needed most. We have to join together, build a successful team, put the plan of action in motion and execute it. This vision Dr. Ware and I have could be the start of changing sickle cell forever in the lives of many.

Epilogue

T.J. Brown's Natural Wellness Story

Before T.J. was born, doctors advised his mother that there was a fifty percent chance he would have sickle cell and urged her to have an abortion so her child would not die young or suffer a lifetime of pain. After much thought and prayer his mother decided to go forward with the pregnancy, and T.J. was born on May 4, 1988. As a baby, his spleen became so large it was removed by the time he was two years of age. Doctors warned his parents he might not live to see 14 years of age.

After living in the United States, T.J. moved to Jamaica for nine years. He remembers getting sickling episodes very few times over the course of those years in Jamaica. Within a month of moving back to the States, complications with his health began to flare. Due to his frequent hospitalizations, it was very difficult for him to stay in school and keep up his grades. His doctors prescribed medications like penicillin, toradol, hydrocodone, hydroxurea, morphine, dilaudid, fentanyl patches, amoxicillin and others. Over time, they all seemed to stop working and just complicated issues for the worse.

Having several close calls with death, after too many dead ends and being hospitalized every other week, T.J. was left with no answers and spent nearly two-thirds of his life being sick and in pain. He thought he was going to die. His hemoglobin was always low, and doctors would just try to give him blood transfusions. After a while he realized his liver and kidneys were struggling from the iron overload. He finally decided to research other ways to treat all his sickle cell symptoms.

Through reading, research and connecting with vegans, health gurus, and holistic doctors like Dr. Charlie Ware, T.J. learned that foods like berries, greens and herbs have been used to treat illnesses such as cancer, diabetes and sickle cell for hundreds, if not thousands, of years. By gaining knowledge of a natural holistic lifestyle, he was able to overcome something he was told would be impossible. He learned that a path that includes natural plant-based nutrition to combat pain, raise the blood count, boost the immune system, and give the red blood cells a longer life span would show real, positive results.

T.J. will be 25 years young soon. Death is a word often connected to sickle cell anemia, but T.J. chose to ignore his prognosis. After his success with his own health, he wanted to share the good news and help people all over the world. In August 2010, T.J. founded Sickle Cell Natural Wellness Group Inc. (SCNWG), a non-profit organization whose mission is to support health advocacy and build global awareness for sickle cell anemia. The organization advocates using natural modalities such as plant-based nutrition, holistic methods and health programs, to alleviate sickle cell pain crisis. The group is dedicated to improving the lives of those living with sickle cell anemia and the sickle cell trait through education and healthy lifestyle choices. SCNWG hosts and participates in meetings, presentations, one-on-one counseling, video productions and interviews, visiting sickle cell patients in the hospital and various activities aimed at helping families and individuals live healthy abundant lives. He has been a featured guest on TBN and at various health seminars, radio stations, hospital support groups, events and community functions. Through SCNWG he has managed to raise funds to provide wellness information and food baskets containing healthy alternatives to families and individuals alike. T.J. is a vegan today and believes it has helped him to live a more fulfilling life without getting sick as he once did in the past.

For more information, to get involved, to donate, or to be a sponsor, contact T.J Brown at http://www.scnwg. org/giving-back.html, sccantstopme@gmail.com, or 561-929-4544.

References

http://www.lifewithgreens.com/why-green-is-good-for-you-chlorophyll

http://www.theoncologyinstitute.com/?pgid=468&parid=457&rid=457

http://learn.genetics.utah.edu/content/disorders/whataregd/sicklecell/

The Mayo Foundation for Medical Education and Research (MFMER) http://www.mayo.edu/

http://www.sickle-thal.nwlh.nhs.uk/ForPatients/KeepingWellWithSickleCellDisease.aspx

www.herbwisdom.com/herb-goldenseal.html

http://clinicaltrials.gov/show/NCT01443728

http://www.naturalnews.com/022851_Colostrum_studies_health.html#ixzz2bhiGO4so

http://health.mo.gov/living/families/genetics/sicklecell/glossary.php

http://sickle.bwh.harvard.edu/hemoglobinopathy.html

http://www.webmd.com/a-to-z-guides/sickle-cell-disease-topic-overview

http://www.gorhams.dk/html/the_lymphatic_system.html

Where to Purchase Herbs
Dr. Charlie Ware, AP, LLC
Acupuncture Herbs Homeopathic and Rehabilitation
Hollywood, FL 33019
http://drcharlieware.com/

Sprouts Farmers Market
http://sprouts.com/

Sickle Cell Foundations/Support Groups
www.ssnaturalhealing.com
Sickle Cell Natural Wellness Group
http://www.scnwg.org/index.html

Sickle Cell National Association of Cameroon
+237 740 318 18

Sickle Cell Disease Association of America/Philadelphia Delaware Valley Chapter
http://sicklecelldisorder.com/

Sickle Cell Information Center
http://scinfo.org/sickle-cell-clinics-contacts-and-resources

The Sickle Cell and Thalassemia Support Group of Barking, Dagenham and Havering
http://www.sicklecellbhr.org.uk/
http://www.sicklecellbhr.org.uk/index.php?option=com_content&view=article&id=33&Itemid=23

Sickle Cell Foundation Nigeria
http://www.sicklecellfoundation.com/index.php

Sickle Cell Disease Foundation of California
http://www.scdfc.org/

Sickle Cell Foundation, Tallahassee, FL
http://sicklecellfoundation.org/

Sickle Cell Miami
http://www.sicklecellmiami.org/

Tamika Moseley

Sickle Cell Disease Association, Southern Connecticut
http://www.scdaaofsouthernct.org/

Sickle Cell Information Center, Atlanta, GA
http://scinfo.org/patients-and-families-patient-care-in-atlanta-ga/the-georgia-comprehensive-sickle-cell-center-at-grady-health-system-in-atlanta-georgia

Acknowledgements

First and foremost, I would like to give thanks to almighty God for directing my steps, leading me on this journey and giving me the passion to care for my family as well as others. He is my rock always and forever. I would like to thank my wonderful husband, Rodney Moseley, for his patience, dedication, and understanding throughout this process, allowing me to live my dream and supporting it to the end—I love you! Thanks to our beautiful children with whom God has blessed us: Mariah, Aiden and Rodney II. A special thanks to my mom "Rose Mosby" for her support and love and raising me to be the person I am today. A special thanks to my wonderful dad (I love you). Thanks to my brothers Rodney Mosby (LaToya Mosby), Colin Kepney (Carla Kepney), Cleavis Kepney (Kathy Kepney). Special thanks to Dr. Charlie Ware for all his hard work and dedication towards this project, and to Dr. Nagaratina Salem and Dr. Roger Tappa and Dr. Tania-White Jackson. Thanks to my wonderful editor, Randy Foster, and to Vanessa Lowry, Victor Guy Aime Dongo for all of his hard work and dedication seeing the trials getting set up, we appreciate you! Stacey Ward, Nico

Toliver, Faith Ogala, Karen Easley, Jackie Rochelle, Jason Moseley (Carla Moseley), Arthur Moseley (Marilou Moseley) Emma Stephen, and Tom from the natural health shop.

About the Author

Tamika Moseley grew up in Shreveport, Louisiana. At the age of 18 she joined the United States Army Reserve and later received an honorable discharge from the military. She received a Bachelor of Science degree in Human Relations and Business from Amberton University in Garland, Texas.

Tamika's purpose in life is being of service to others. She is a member of Greenville Avenue Church of Christ in Richardson, Texas, where she serves on the Benevolence and Missionary teams. Because her son has sickle cell disease, she has a huge passion to help others in this fight. She wants to share her amazing story with other parents and all who suffer from this disease. Tamika's current focus is teaming up with Dr. Charlie Ware and aiding the sickle cell battle in Africa, where the disease is so prominent. Their main goal is to provide education, guidance and useful information on the importance of natural herbs and how they can help sustain our health while living with sickle cell disease. Tamika and her husband Rodney, and their three beautiful children, live in Dallas, TX.